Items should be returned on or before the last date shown below. Items not already requested by other borrowers may be renewed in person, in writing or by telephone. To renew, please quote the number on the barcode label. To renew online a PIN is required. This can be requested at your local library.
Renew online @ **www.dublincitypubliclibraries.ie**
Fines charged for overdue items will include postage incurred in recovery. Damage to or loss of items will be charged to the borrower.

Leabharlanna Poiblí Chathair Bhaile Átha Cliath
Dublin City Public Libraries

Du

Dublin City
Baile Átha Cliath

RINGSEND BRANCH TEL. 6680063

Pro

Date Due	Date Due	Date Due

D1513598

Archbishop Richard Whately (1787-1863)

Liam O' Meara

Within & Without...

Dublin Churches of St. Nicholas

And exploring the Manx connection

RIPOSTE BOOKS DUBLIN

2008

First Published by *RIPOSTE BOOKS,* 2008
28 Emmet Rd Dublin 8. Ireland

ISBN: 978-1-901596-14-4

Printed by BETAPRINT

Cover Illustrations
Front: *St Nicholas of Myra*, stained glass window by Earley & Co.
Back: St Nicholas Within, photographed by the author

Contents

Appendix

Dedication

*With special thanks to John Gallagher, John Brogan, Bernard Warfield and the members of the **Liberties Living Heritage**, 2008.*

Illustrations   page

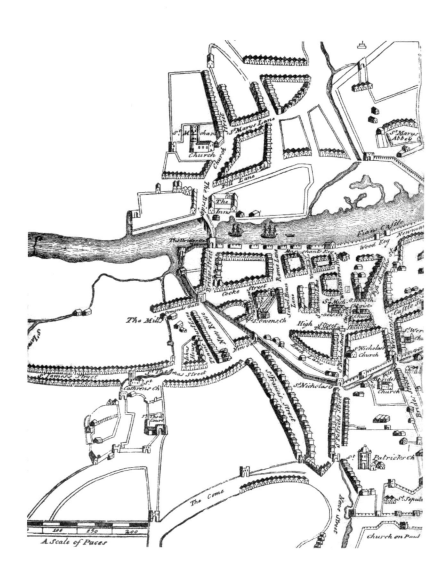

John Speed's Map of Dublin, 1610

8

Foreword

The terms, St. Nicholas Within and St. Nicholas Without have been for many years a source of amusement to Dubliners; and in the main, it is only Dubliners who know of their origins. They apply to the churches built, respectively, inside and outside the walls of the city. Nicholas Street was originally separated from Patrick's Street by a gate in the city wall, known as St. Nicholas' Gate. On the top of this gate the Parliamentarians, in their time, impaled the head of Luke O'Tuathal, of Castlekevin, Wicklow, chief of the clan of O'Tuathail, who was the first to levy troops in Leinster to defend Charles I against the Puritans. The gate and walls were described thus:

" St. Nicholas'-gate have towe rounde towres withowt and sqware within, and the said gate placed betwixte bothe the towres, every towre three heightes, whereof two loftes, and fowre lowpes in every towre; the wall five foote thicke, thirty-nine foote in lengthe one waye, and eighteen foote brode the other waye, and the towre forty-fyve foot hie, with a perculles [portcullis] for the same gate."[i]

St. Nicholas Within, once the smallest parish in Dublin, only a little over five acres, and St. Nicholas Without, a long narrow strip between New Street and the river Poddle, eventually one of the largest parishes, are both of great antiquity. Of the former church, all that remains today are the outer, ground level walls, the northern of which with its five bricked up windows is at the rear of 'the Millennium Garden,' or Peace Park, a project launched in 1988 and opened by the Lord Mayor, Cllr. Ben Briscoe. This wall originally overlooked a tiny graveyard and possibly had six windows before the widening of the streets in 1911, when the west front was moved back several feet.[ii] The west wall is still clearly visible on the corner of Nicholas Street and Christ Church Place. At the entrance to the garden is a fine piece of bronze street sculpture titled, *The Millennium Child*, by John Behan, depicting three children of the Millennium. It was sponsored by Barnadoes, and unveiled by President Mary MacAleese, in 2000.

Of the latter Church, the North Transept of St. Patrick's Cathedral today shows no sign of the chapel that once represented the parish of St. Nicholas Without; nor is there any trace of the church at Limerick Lane or the old Franciscan chapel which gave its name to Francis Street. However, there is the splendid Church of St. Nicholas of Myra, on the same site. It must be said though, that the terms Within and Without do not sufficiently cover the complicated nature of the churches of the parishes of St. Nicholas. The main function of this present study is to separate the Roman Catholic history from the Church of Ireland history, and to shed some light on the curious connection of the Isle of Man with the diocese of Francis Street.

In 1873, a marriage took place at St. Nicholas of Myra Church between Mary Ann Dalton and John Miara. Mary Anne was from a well known family in the Bride Street area who kept a shoe warehouse; John Miara (the name written by the clerk) was a boot maker from Clare who had come to Dublin. Mary Anne and John met, and John never returned to his home in Killaloe. They had several children whom they raised in various tenements in the Bride Street and Bishop Street areas. The first children were christened with the surname Mara and the later children O' Meara. Mary-Ann and John were my greatgrandparents. I, myself was born at Ussher's Quay, and, having no garden, my parents often took me to play in St. Patrick's Park where the only photograph of my sister was taken; she died in infancy. Many Dublin families at that time used the park for photo shoots. With St. Patrick's being such a tourist attraction today, the park is always thronged with photographers.

My sources are listed in the Appendix section, but in presenting this book, I would like to personally acknowledge certain people for their help and encouragement: Fr. Paul Kenny, Administrator, Martin Dolan, Curate, Rita Kavanagh, Sacristan- St. Nicholas of Myra Parish Church; Frances Crowley, historian, Peel, Isle of Man; Ken Mc Gowan, Theresa Whitington, The Central Catholic Lending Library; Dominick Dowling; Patricia Quigley, The Jesuit Library, Dublin; the Dean and guides of St. Patrick's Cathedral; The British Museum; Alderman John Gallagher; the Liberties Living Heritage 2008, especially Jane Devereaux; The Gilbert Library; and all the staff (my friends) at The National Library of Ireland .-

Liam O' Meara,   July, 2008

11

The Church of St. Nicholas Within as illustrated in 'The Gentlemen's Magazine' 1786.

St. Nicholas Within

St. Nicholas Within

Donat, Bishop of Dublin, with the assistance of Sitric, the Danish king of Dublin, erected the Cathedral of the Holy Trinity, or Christ Church, about the year 1038. It is believed that he was also responsible for the earliest church dedicated to St. Nicholas, the patron saint of mariners. This church was situated on the north side of the Cathedral and is thought to have served as a beacon to the Norsemen as they sailed up the river Liffey, which was not contained at the time and spread further to the North and South. Sometime in the 12th century a new church was built on the present site on higher ground within the protected area of the walled city. Then in the 14th century, the parish was extended beyond the walls and the north transept of St. Patrick's Cathedral became the parish church of St. Nicholas Without.

St. Nicholas Within was restored in 1578, and entirely rebuilt in 1707. The exterior stone was of very dark colour, called black slate or calp. It consisted of three stories gradually diminishing in breadth to the summit. A good description was recorded by John James McGregor in 1821:

'The present church of St. Nicholas Within was erected in the year 1707. Its front is of hewn stone, with a large arched door-case in the centre, over which, in the first storey, is a large arched window, with a smaller arched window on each side. In the second storey is another arched window, immediately under the roof of the church. Over this rises a square belfry 12 or 14 feet above the roof with openings on each side. This church if placed in another situation, would make a respectable appearance; but is completely covered in the north and east, and partly so on the south side, by the houses that are built up against it, The west end which is the front faces to Nicholas street, which is here so narrow that a stranger, in passing, can hardly take notice of the church; if it should attract his attention, he cannot view its structure without inconvenience. The Dean and Chapter of St. Patrick's have the appointment of a curate to this parish.'[iii]

This description resembles the illustration that appeared in the *Gentleman's Magazine* in 1786. Both St. Nicholas Without and St Nicholas Within were at his time small and poor:

'The parish was the smallest in Dublin, but because of its central situation was the abode of many of the more wealthy shop-keepers. In 1814, there were only 102 houses and 1447 inhabitants. Beside the church once stood the Tholsel,[*] a massy and not inelegant stone edifice, deriving its name from the old words "toll- stall," i.e. the toll-gatherer's stall or seat, being the place where the collectors attended to receive the toll or custom for such goods as were liable to the city imposts.'[iv]

The church built in 1707 would be the last church built in this parish and would serve for only 128 years. Neglect owing to lack of funding would be its downfall. Apart from minor repairs to the steeple in 1775 and 1819, no other work was carried out on the building. In 1821, the same year as Mc Gregor's observations which avoided all mention of decline, a sad portrayal was given by fellow historian, George Newenham Wright:

'(St. Nicholas Within) …is of a gloomy, uninteresting appearance and the front is inclined so much from perpendicularity as to be exceedingly dangerous. The interior is miserable in the extreme; the pews falling to decay, the walls and ceiling in a wretched condition, and the organ is very old and weak-toned. There is a gallery at the west end, which only accommodates the children of the parish school. The cemetery was formerly sufficiently large in proportion to the extent of the parish, but the corporation purchased the major part of it to erect the Tholsel upon, and now

---

*The late medieval merchants' hall, known as the Tholsel, stood at the top of Nicholas Street just north of the present ruins of St. Nicholas's Church. By the middle of the fifteenth century the Tholsel accommodated the town clock, wich was probably the first public mechanical clock of its kind in Ireland. The same building housed the Chain Book which was attached by a chain for security and could be consulted on the laws and usage of the town.

it is reduced to such scanty dimensions as to be merely a passage to the vaults. In these vaults several persons of high descent have been deposited; but their names can be learned only from the parish register, as there are no monuments to mark the spot were they are laid.'[v]

By 1835, it was found to be in an unsafe *"ruinous and unroofed"* condition. Even demolition proved costly, with some church items having to be sold off to meet payment of bills. The Dean and Chapter of St. Patrick's, who had not been consulted prior to the sale, were understandably annoyed. They had heard *"with surprise and indignation that materials and the furniture of the church had been disposed of; the pews to the proprietor of a whiskey shop or public house and the Communion Table and altarpiece and windows have been sold for the use of a new Popish Chapel in County Dublin..."* [vi] In the event, the Communion Table was not sold, but deposited with the verger at the Cathedral.

With no church, the parishioners worshipped for a time at the Cathedral along with the faithful of St. Nicholas Without, in the chapel in the North transept, then Anglicized, of course. The newly appointed, Archbishop Richard Whately inquired of one of his clergy *"What is this St. Nicholas Within Without?"* Having being given a full account, he replied with his usual wit, *"Now we understand. We have a St. Nicholas Within without a church and a St. Nicholas Without within a church!"*[vii] Later, in 1846, it was Archbishop Whately who licensed the schoolhouse beside the old roofless church as a place of worship. A contemporary observer has left us this vivid word picture:

'How shall we account for the scandal of St. Nicholas Within- a sham parish of five acres, adjoining Christ Church Cathedral, with only a street between? ...There is located upon the five acres which this unique parish contains, a total population of 1,838, of which 184 belong to the Established Church...if any one is curious to find the parish church of St. Nicholas Within upon a Sunday at noon, he will, after diligent inquiry, be directed to a small house adjoining the ruins of the church. He ascends a narrow staircase...till he sees two little rooms thrown into one with forms to seat twenty five or thirty persons. Beside the stairs there is a box, serving as a

15

pulpit and reading desk and immediately under it a small table for the Holy Communion. Beside the pulpit is an old easy chair for the clerk, a comfortable-looking man in plaid slippers, who seems from his manner to be fully sensible of the comicality of the situation, and to enjoy it thoroughly...not more than twenty persons constituted the congregation, for which two clergy do duty in a garret- as mean as any room I have ever seen used by Methodist home missionaries for village prayer meetings...the present Archbishop of Dublin and his Archdeacon, hearing the fame of this church, dropped in one day to see it, and one can easily understand how shocking to their refined ecclesiastical taste...?'[viii]

Notwithstanding the claustrophobic nature of the facility, Sunday service was held there regularly until 1867, when the parish was united with St. Audoen's.

No history of this parish would be complete without mention of the redoubtable, Tresham Dames Gregg, a controversialist with extreme views in Protestantism. His grandfather of the same name, according to tradition, was the governor of Newgate prison who served Robert Emmet his last breakfast in 1803.[ix] Young Tresham studied at Trinity College, Dublin, where he made a name for himself as a profound scholar of Hebrew and an able mathematician. He was ordained a deacon in the diocese of Ossory in 1828, and thereafter identified himself with militant churchmen who were opposed to Roman Catholicism. Though appalled by the poverty of the Irish peasantry, his evangelical beliefs led him to conclude that this was all the fault of Rome and that such calamities as the cholera of 1832 and, later, the famine were divine judgments. He came to prominence in 1838, when he was involved in a marathon debate with his Catholic counterpart, controversialist, Thomas Maguire and was the apparent champion. This brought him a strong working-class Protestant following. In 1840, he further developed his evangelical skills as the chosen chaplain of Swift's Alley Church.

Then, in 1842, by what seems suspiciously like a set-up, Tresham, or "Thrash 'em Gregg," as he was known for his prowess in the pulpit, was led to believe that a young Protestant woman had been kidnapped and taken to a convent. In a moment of haste rivaling the

16

actions of the ill-fated Lord of Kildare, he visited the convent and demanded the immediate release of the woman. It turned out, however, that she was a willing convert who had already pledged herself as a bride of Christ and so, had no need of this Don Quixote rescue attempt. A crowd gathered and pelted him with stones; he was further, detained in the Bridewell for a week, despite a robust defense by Isaac Butt. Archbishop Whately, wishing to avoid sectarian tensions with Roman Catholicism was acutely embarrassed by the affair and inhibited Gregg from preaching. Tresham had no choice but to resign his position as chaplain of Swift's Alley Church. His loyal Protestant parishioners then used an ancient prerogative, free of Episcopal jurisdiction, to elect him as chaplain of the chantry of St. Mary in the parish of St. Nicholas Within.[*] He had the good fortune to be unaffected by the disestablishment of the Church of Ireland (in 1870), having being appointed prior to disestablishment and was therefore entitled to receive his salary from the estate, valued at the time at £325 per annum. Here he preached well into senility, much to annoyance of Archbishop Whately [#] holding the position to his death forty years later. Among his many deeds was the formation of the Protestant Operatives Association, which had many Orange contacts and sympathies, in opposition to O'Connell's Repeal movement. Despite a "divine disclosure,"[x] which he claimed was made to him in 1866, that he was immortal, the bold chaplain was called to account in 1881. He was the last chaplain of St. Mary's. After his death, the Chantry estate was confiscated by the Church commissioners.

---

[*] This chantry had origins dating back to the time of Edward IV (1461-1483), who granted the Earl of Worcester permission to found a chantry at St.Nicholas Within dedicated to god and the Blessed Virgin. The founders were allowed to purchese property to the value of £13 for support of a chaplain elected by the parishoners. Following the suppression of the monasteries and various acts of parliament this chantry was probably the only one to survive almost to the twentieth century.

[#] Anglican Archbishop, Richard Whatley was an interesting man of high particulary fond of puns. He was liberal towards the Roman Catholics to Outwardly, he adopted the stance taht the impoverished state of the Irish the only solution. However, privately he donated some £8, 000 for relief during the harsh 1846-1849 period. Questions of tithes, reform of the Irish church and of the Irish Poor Laws, and, in particular, the organization of national education occupied much of his time. He discussed other public questions, for example, the subject of transportation and the general question of secondary punishments.

position to his death forty years later. Among his many deeds was the formation of the Protestant Operatives Association, which had many Orange contacts and sympathies, in opposition to O'Connell's Repeal movement. Despite a "divine disclosure,"[x] which he claimed was made to him in 1866, that he was immortal, the bold chaplain was called to account in 1881. He was the last chaplain of St. Mary's. After his death, the Chantry estate was confiscated by the Church commissioners.

St. Nicholas Without
(Pre- Reformation)

The first church of St. Nicholas without was said to be at Limerick Alley, between Francis Street and Patrick's Street. In the mid 1300s the parish was extended to beyond the walls of the city to include the Liberty of St. Sepulchre's Palace and the Liberty of St. Patrick's Deanery. For 500 years the north transept of the Cathedral of St. Patrick, built by Archbishop Comyn in 1190, was used as the parish church of St. Nicholas Without. Archbishop John Alen later commented that St. Nicholas's was, *"...a double Church- one within the walls of the city and the other within St. Patrick Cathedral; both are small and poor ."[xi]* St. Nicholas Without was fitted with galleries, pulpit and altar, and a wall partitioned the north transept from the rest of the cathedral. William Brereton, in his travels in Ireland, gave this account:

'In a corner, a small part of the middle aisle, there is a pretty neat convenient place wherein there is a sermon every Sabbath at ten hour, and this, though it be very little and narrow, yet is sufficiently enlarged to receive a great congregation by reason of capacious galleries around about wherein are abundance of seats placed one above another with great advantage of room.'

By 1707, the population, owing largely to the influx of Huguenots, who also used a part of the cathedral, had grown to the extent that it was decided to divide the parish. By Act of Parliament made in that year, the part of the parish known by the name of the Donore district (then the Coombe area) was detached from it and in 1708, formed into a new parish, under the name of St. Luke's. A church, often referred to as 'the poplin church of Luke's,' was built by John

Lady Chapel (1860's): The 'French Church,' used by St. Nicholas Without

Whimrey in 1714. By 1784, the north transept of St Patrick's fell into decline, mainly from regular flooding by the river Poddle, and remained in ruins for almost 40 years. During this period the parishioners met in another part of the cathedral, St Mary's, (commonly called the 'French church,' having been set to the French congregation.) and for which parishioners paid an annual rent of £30. Both parishes had close associations with the Huguenot refugees who had settled in the area in the late 17th century and an amalgamation seemed inevitable. On the 1st February 1789, the parishioners of St, Nicholas Without and of St. Luke's met under the same roof. During that year, in a gesture of solidarity they donated £90 towards the building of a new gallery to accommodate the extra numbers in St. Luke's Church. Disagreements, unfortunately, soon arose between the two vestries apparently over finances and in the early 1790's the parishioners of St. Nicholas returned to the Cathedral where they once more rented the French Church.

From 1784-1793, collections were made for restoration purposes at the Cathedral, but it was not until 1822-26, that work was carried out on the north transept and it was re-roofed. Service thereafter, reverted to here, but unfortunately, no part of this reconstruction has survived. By 1860, the north transept was again in need of repairs and a complete rebuilding project was undertaken by Guinness founder, Sir Benjamin Lee Guinness, 1861-65. In the course of the work, the partition was removed and the Cathedral returned to a more cruciform shape. It was decided to amalgamate the parish of St. Nicholas Without permanently with that of St. Luke's; the latter on the Coombe, to be the parish church for both. The final service of St. Nicholas Without in the Cathedral was on 20th October 1861.

St. Nicholas and St. Luke's, as it was.

St. Nicholas Without & St. Luke's

While the history of these times involves a period when Roman Catholics were suppressed, it is ironic that the Huguenots (non-Episcopal Calvinists), fled here in the late 17th century to avoid persecution in Catholic France. Those who conformed to the Episcopal church, were accommodated in the Lady Chapel of St Patrick's Cathedral. By 1708, the population had swollen owing to the success of the weaving trade and with the arrival of more immigrants, such as Dutch and Flemish Protestants. Areas such as, Spitalfields, and Pimlico are reminders of the many London Huguenot families who were once lured here. For the 12,172 inhabitants at this time, principally of the poorest class, there were only 980 houses. At church too, the overcrowding was causing problems. In 1707, a new parish was formed south of the Coombe between two channels of the Poddle river running down Crooked Staff on the west and up the Blackpitts on the east. Then in 1715 a separate Church and Glebe house were built. There was a graveyard attached, but few Huguenots were buried there, preferring, it seems, to be laid alongside their relatives at "the Cabbage Garden," adjoining the Lady chapel at the Cathedral. This rather humorous moniker dates to the time of Oliver Cromwell (1649-1660) whose soldiers rented the ground to grow cabbages.[#]

It is rightfully said that the Huguenots brought much needed employment, but equally, the area became solely dependent on the silk and poplin trades. The industry flourished in the 18th. century, but began to decline by the early part of 19th century. In 1861, the parish was united again with that of St. Nicholas Without. This proved to be a mistake as there was constant discord between the two

---

[#] Situated at the end of Cathedral Lane, off Kevin street. Today it is a park, but some of the headstones can still be seen.

parishes. Eventually the Protestant population dwindled and so did trade, bringing much poverty to the area. The Liberties soon became notorious for its slums, said to be among the worst in Europe; a condition which lasted into the twentieth century.

There were many alterations and additions made to the church throughout the years, including: a replacement pulpit; the construction of a classically articulated chancel with a barrel vault; a new semi-circular window depicting *Christ calming the storm;* a new stone altar and the replacement of the previous compass ceiling by a flat compartmentalized one.[xii] The window was one of the best remembered features of the church and was donated, in 1902, by the family of Ellen Parkes, wife of the hardware merchant whose premises was nearby.[*] A new bell commemorating the arrival of the Huguenots in 1685 and fashioned out of two original bells dating to 1714, was presented to the church by John Newman together with a belfry in 1903. Fortunately, the bell survived the closure of the church and can now be seen at the north transept, St. Patrick's Cathedral. The inscription reads:

'To the glory of God and in the memory of the coming of the Huguenots 1685.'

The final service at St Luke's was held on the occasion of the Harvest Thanksgiving on the 19th September 1975. The church was then deconsecrated and closed, thus ending the Protestant connection with St. Nicholas in Dublin. Local Dubliners, anxious to preserve their heritage campaigned to save the church. However, as always, there was general apathy with the authorities regarding non-Catholic churches; those not bull-dozed being sold for commercial use, regardless of their architectural or historical interest. St. Luke's was used for a short time as a publishing house and then left idle.

---

[*] Later returned to the family on the closure of the church

The Historic Cabbage Garden, Huguenot Graveyard, today a park.

The final service at St Luke's was held on the occasion of the Inevitably, in 1986, a gang broke into the crypt and a number of coffins were left exposed; one actually set alight. Later that same year, a fire in the church left only a smoldering ruin. In 1990, the Representative Church Body sold the church, subject to a covenant outlining conditions for future use, for a peppercorn fee of £5 to the then Dublin Corporation. In 2002, a relief road opened at the rear of the church and the following year construction began on the Widow's Alms House,[*] next door. In 2005, St. Luke's Conservation plan was launched by Dublin City Council in conjunction with the Heritage Council. This confirmed St. Luke's status as a protected building and outlined proposals for the reuse of the church and the landscaping of surrounding areas:

'In accordance with statuary obligations pertaining to the protected structure status of St. Luke's, that the surviving structure of the Church should be retained and restored, including the external walls, window and door ops, the ground floor nave, the east chancel and the crypts. ..... That the sacred nature of the site as a burial ground is respected in any future use of St. Luke's especially the grounds.'[xiii]

There was even the suggestion that the original bell, now in the care of the Church of Ireland, should be returned when the bellcote is restored. The latest report on this development, however, is very disappointing. Locals had hoped that the building could be used as a much needed heritage centre and for back-to-work training courses. Sadly, it seems it will be turned into offices and apartments like so many other treasured sites which are today but painted facades that simply remind us of what we have lost. It will therefore be of little practical use to this community. A well chosen quote of Walter Benjamin, used in the published *St. Luke's Conservation Plan,* is sadly ringing true:

'Every trace of the past that is not recognized in the present threatens to disappear irretrievably.'[xiv]

---

[*] A tall narrow building, three storeys high, built as a parochial school in the early 19th. Century (Lewis-1837). The well known lettering to the frontage was added circa 1880. Ten windows lived here in 1942.

St. Nicholas Without and St. Luke's. Also the Widows Alms House.

Silken Thomas at St. Mary's Abbey, and the Siege of Dublin 1534

Catholics Since the Reformation

From the time of the English Reformation life was very different for the Catholic communities of the parishes of St. Nicholas, as indeed it was for Catholics generally. When St. Patrick's was Anglicized, they had used the church at the Monastery of St. Francis. It may be of interest here to give a little history of this monastery before we continue.

The site on which the present church is built appears to have been a place of worship from at least the 12th. century when a timber church existed there. In 1235, Ralph Le Porter, son of the High Provost of Dublin gave lands outside the city walls to the Grey Friars or Franciscans. They built a convent on grounds after which, Francis Street was named. The friary had many benefactors, including Henry III, who issued a liberate on 8th. October, 1236 authorizing payment of 10 marks to "*forward the building of their Convent, in the suburbs of Dublin*". [*]

In 1305, the King's secretary, Michael Le Browne, Knight, died in Ireland and was interred here. The funeral was attended with '*more solemnity and a greater number of wax lights than was ever before witnessed on a similar occasion in Ireland.*' [xv] John Le Decer, who was Mayor of Dublin, erected a beautiful chapel in honour of the Blessed Virgin Mary in 1308; he was laid to rest there in 1332. In 1309, Roger Le Hatton, guardian of the Franciscan Order in Dublin and Walter Prendergast, a lecturer of the same order, were examined as witnesses to the charge laid against the Knights Templars and that same year a provincial Chapter of the order was held. The Black Plaque swept through Ireland in 1348 bringing death to 140,000 Dubliners among whom were 24 friars.

---

[*] From the Parish Register

29

In 1534, Silken Thomas made an assault on the city and tried to breach the New-gate, but was foiled by the skill and bravery of the townsmen:

'Among his army were a number of inhabitants of the Pale, on whom, as compulsory followers of his standard, the citizens counted as secretly friends to their cause. In this cheering hope they were further confirmed, on finding that the arrows shot over the walls were most of them without heads, and that some even conveyed letters giving information of the besiegers' designs. These encouraging circumstances led them to resolve upon a sally; and, having given out from the walls that new succours had arrived from England, they rushed forth, through fire and flame, on the ranks of the enemy, who, judging from this boldness that the rumoured reinforcements had actually arrived, immediately fled, leaving one hundred of their gallowglasses slain, and most of their cannon in the hands of the citizens. FitzGerald himself lay hid all night at the Friary in Francis Street, and from thence escaped, at break of day, to his camp.'[xvi]

When St. Patrick's Cathedral was Anglicized in 1537, most of the population of the surrounding Pale remained Roman Catholic; the faithful seeking refuge at the Franciscan Abbey. Henry VIII's pillaging of religious houses, however, soon reached Dublin and, in 1540 his soldiers took possession of the monastery at Francis Street. These holdings and lands were granted to Thomas Stephens, a Dublin merchant and former proctor of the church. At the time, they were described as consisting of the Monastery itself- church, bell-tower, dormitory hall, 3 chambers cemetery and garden and four messuages- together with three gardens in Francis Street and six acres of meadows near Clondalkin; to be held in capite at the annual rent of two shillings. His family retained title rights until the end of the 16th century. By 1617, no trace remained of the old monastery.

In 1616, Dr. Eugene Mathews created the parish of St Nicholas, to include the chapels of St Bride, St Michael Le Pol, St. Kevin, St. Peter, St. Stephen, and St. Andrew. Worship, of course was a different matter, with the bishop himself lucky to escape his persecutors on more than one occasion. In the reign of Charles I and his Catholic Queen, Henrietta Maria, some chapels were erected, but there was no place in Francis Street at this time. The Cromwellian Period, again dealt the progress of Catholics a severe blow and it was not until after the Restoration of King Charles II, in 1660 that there was any respite. A Franciscan friar, Fr. Barnwall of the community in Cook street seized the opportunity to rebuild the ancient monastery in Francis Street. He was a member an influential and affluent family and was able to raise the funds to obtain the site. He began with the rebuilding of the chapel, but before he had advanced any further, the Titus Oates persecution (1675) spread to Ireland and halted the work. The so-called, "Popish plot" was a total fabrication involving the proposed assassination of the King and some leading Protestant gentlemen. The hysteria generated by Oates (for his own personal financial and social gain) led to the execution of many innocent Catholics, including (Saint) Oliver Plunkett, Archbishop of Armagh. The Franciscans were glad to pass the property and buildings over to the secular clergy, who up to this time were using a ramshackle chapel in Limerick Alley,* a narrow strip between Nicholas Street and Francis Street, (now closed up.)

The Franciscan chapel remained incomplete until 1688 (the reign of King James II,) when it was finished and opened for public worship. Access was from Francis Street via an arched entry and a narrow laneway. It was further described thus:

'The chapel is a plain oblong building, 80 x 40 ft. The altar piece, four pillars, and steps are of Kilkenny marble. It is adorned with pictures of the Assumption, St. Peter, St. Paul, St. Patrick, St. Nicholas and St. Thomas. The decorations are the same as in Liffey Street Chapel. Near the pulpit is a statue of St. Anthony of Padua. The choir is above stairs, and the dormitory of the friars serves now as a dwelling place for the priests.[xvii] ,

The chapel at Francis Street was the pro-cathedral church of ten

---

* According to tradition, but "unsupported by any documentary evidence" - Donnelly, *Dublin Parishes.*

successive Archbishops, the first of which was Archbishop Patrick Russell. Their fortunes varied with the political situation, sometimes favourable, and more often not. Dr. Russell, a native of Dublin, was the first victim; a forgotten martyr, for the circumstances in which he died are rarely discussed. The advent of a Catholic King had raised the hopes of the afflicted Catholics of Ireland and with liberty restored to the Church a provincial synod was assembled in 1685, another in 1688; in 1686 and 1689 diocesan synods were held. The metropolitan chapter was reorganized and the precedence of its members settled. A great challenge however, occurred following the disastrous defeat of the Jacobite army and the flight of King James II. This seemed to put an end to all hope, leaving Catholics in a worse situation than ever. Dr. Russell was apprehended and is thought to have suffered much "harassment" before being cast into a filthy underground prison in Dublin, where he died in 1692.

The Bishops continued to use St Nicholas's as their mensal parish, but usually were forced to rule through an administrator; or a parish priest, as in the case of Archdeacon, Thomas Austin 1709-1740.The Archbishop at this time being otherwise engaged:
'Fr. Edmund Byrne, was appointed Archbishop in 1707 (until 1723). The fact that he was consecrated in Newgate Prison by two bishops, Dr. O' Donnelly and Dr. O'Rourke, who were also prisoners there is a telling commentary on the times.'[xviii]

Permission to erect Catholic chapels was not given until 1725 and by 1770, there were twelve chapels in the city. In view of the foregoing, it is surprising to find that a service was held in St. Nicholas Without, in 1789 to give thanksgiving for the return to health of King George III. Archbishop Troy, three bishops, orchestra, choir, soloists, the Duke of Leinster and nine other peers, six MPs including, Thomas Conoly and Henry Grattan, the Lord Mayor and Sheriffs and many more were in attendance, along with an estimated 3,000 people.[xix] Dr. Troy O.P.,(1787-1797) was the last Archbishop to use Francis Street as a Pro-Cathedral, or 'Metropolitan Chapel'. His disposition favoured authority and he was ready to condemn all violent efforts for reform. He frequently grappled with the

"Whiteboys" and sternly denounced them. It was not that he had any sympathy with oppression, but he had lived so long in Rome and had left Ireland at such an early age, that he did not quite understand the condition of things at home, and did not fully appreciate the extent of misery and oppression in which the poor Catholic masses lived. In 1797, he issued a sentence of excommunication against all those of his flock who would join the rebellion. While some priests had defied the ban, less than 60 of approximately 1800, or just three per cent gave support. Some paid a heavy price. On Christmas Day, 1797, a priest was murdered in Kildare because the Government was informed he had exhorted his congregation to "abstain from disloyalty:"[xx]

' He was also one of the most determined supporters of the Union. In 1799, he agreed to accept the veto of government on the appointment of Irish bishops; and even when the other bishops, finding that they had been tricked by Pitt and Castlereagh, repudiated the veto, Dr. Troy continued to support it.'[xxi]

In 1803, a committee formed by Archbishop Troy bought Lord Annesley's house on the corner of Marlborough Street and Elephant Lane (Cathedral Street), within sight of O'Connell Street, as the location for the new Pro-Cathedral. It opened in 1825 and was the first Catholic Episcopal seat established anywhere in the United Kingdom since the reformation. This ended the Pro-Cathedral status and direct involvement of the bishops with the Francis Street site. The circuit of the parish at this time was the most extensive of any belonging to the metropolis. In addition to the parish of St. Nicholas Without, it encompassed St. Luke's, St. Bride's, St. Kevin's, a part of St. Peter's, and extended to Donnybrook road, on the south-east, and in a south and south-west direction taking in the villages of Mount Pleasant, Ranelagh, Milltown, Rathmines, Roundtown and Harold's Cross, etc. The parochial duties were executed by the parish priest, who was also R.C. Dean of Dublin, and eight assistant curates.[xxii]

The new Roman Catholic Church, Francis Street, Dublin.

The original of St. Nicholas of Myra Parish Church

34

The Church of St. Nicholas of Myra

The Rev. Matthew Flanagan (born in Smithfield, Dublin and formerly of St Catherine's, Meath Street,1809) became parish priest here in 1827, and decided to alter the existing church which was too small for the growing population. In the end he decided to build a totally new church. The present church of St. Nicholas of Myra was designed by John Leeson. Building began in 1829 and lasted until 1834, when the doors finally opened to the public. It was claimed that Leeson mapped out the principal lines etc., and that the finishing touches were all Fr. Flanagan's ideas.[**] The frontage, as we know it today, differs from the original plan as shown in the etching published in the Dublin Penny Journal of 1832, [#]and which was criticized in the same journal as being:

'...an incongruous association of a Gothic spire rising out of a Greek portico-a union which destroys the effect of both, and which is at variance with every principal of correct taste.'

The proposed frontage was changed and in place of the spire a "copper pudding-bowl dome,"[*] actually a clock tower and copper cupola, together with a Quadra style Ionic portico were later erected by Fr. MacCabe, in 1856-1860. The architect was, John Bourke and the cost was £5,000. The church is set back from the street facing onto a small courtyard entered by some simple gates, even though at the time of building there was no longer any law prohibiting a front opening: this was for historical reasons. A description of the new church is contained in one of the old parish registers. It is said to be:

'A true copy of notices engrossed in parchment enclosed in a bottle with the coins of the day and laid in a stone under the great altar of the Church- Matthew Flanagan, P.P. December 1st. 1834.'

** According to the Parish register of 1834
# Vol. 27, Dec.29 th. 1832, pp 213
* as described by Maurice Craig in 'Dublin 1660-1860.'

(Extract)

'This new Roman Catholick Church of St. Nicholas Without stands on the site of the old chapel, an oblong building 80 by 40 feet, where also stood the Monastery of St. Francis built in 1235. The remains of Michael le Brown Secretary of Edward 1ˢᵗ, and probably the ancestor of the present Landlord Capt. Brown of the Family of Castle-Brown, were buried here in 1305 and afterwards the remains of John le Decer, Mayor of the City were buried in the Chapel of St. Mary which he had erected and the ruins of which stood on the South side of the present Church in the passage between the Church and the new Presbytery.

The new Church is an imperfect cross from head to foot in the clear 125 feet transept 82 by 40 feet. The foot of the Cross or Nave 80 by 42 feet in height 43 feet vaulted ceiling the centre over the transept a truncated dome with 3 vaults for burial underneath each 40 by 20 feet 12 feet in height. The remains of the late pastor the Rev. Richard Kenrick were removed from the Cathedral and deposited under the great altar near which lie the remains of the Mother and Brother of the present Pastor the Revd. Matthew Flanagan. The building was commenced January 1829 and now to be completed interiorly before January next will cost £8,400 of which the poor and labouring classes collected by a Society of the undernamed ᵗcharitable individuals during the space of five years with unremitting and indefatigable zeal amounted to £2,959.5.5. the remainder was supplied by the donations of the Richer Parishioners, of the Parish Clergy and of certain Charitable Individuals residing out of the parish.'*

In her recent book on the buildings of Dublin, author Christine Casey recounts that, in Fr. Flanagan's time, the gallery once collapsed

---

Full list included in the register

* Original spelling, (lack of) punctuation and capitalization. Some passages are difficult to decipher.

killing a number of people. This is slightly inaccurate. To discover what really happened, we must examine the news reports from that time. The following is from the Freeman's Journal :

'Appalling Catastrophe and Outrage ^{xxiii}'

A circumstance of a most fatal and horrifying nature took place yesterday morning (Christmas Day) in the Catholic Church of St. Nicholas Without, Francis Street. It appears, according to the best accounts which we have been able to collect from eye-witnesses, that at the first mass which was celebrated, according to custom on that festival, at six o clock in the morning an alarm was given by some ruffian or ruffians that the gallery was falling; and the inhuman miscreant who originated the cry, at the same instant broke a stick, which he had concealed about him, to make it appear that one of the beams had cracked. This took place at the most solemn period of the sacrifice- the church being at the time densely crowded- and in a moment, a scene of indescribable confusion ensued. Some unfortunate people jumped from the gallery and a dreadful rush was made by all towards the doors; a great number were trampled under foot and severely injured, and we hear with pain that five of six have died of their bruises. Some add to the number and others diminish it: but at the same time we have not had a opportunity of ascertaining the facts with certainty, one thing appears certain, that human life has been sacrificed. We hear that the demon by whom this scene of horror was produced is known and does not belong to the communion whose service he disturbed in so fearful a manner. We hope that he may be visited with just retribution. We have been requested to publish the following document, which, however, we do not think to have been called for, as there was evidently no foundation for the dreadful alarm which was caused:-'

"Having minutely examined the gallery of the Roman Catholic Church of St. Nicholas Without , and all the parts connected with it, we found every part in the most permanent state, without any indication of the slightest failure, and we are satisfied that no possible number of persons that the gallery is capable of containing could occasion the least injury to it.

> *John Leeson, Architect*
> *William Sweeney, Builder*
> *December, 25th 1840."*

The coroner's inquest, held a few days later revealed that the deed was not as premeditated as to allow for the culprit bringing a stick with him with deliberate intent. The stick was found to be from a collection of building materials, stored in a corner of the church by a stone-mason, who was working there that week. It was likely, therefore, that the individual saw the stick, and in a mad moment devised the scheme.

Fr. Matthew Flanagan P.P., died on the 28th April 1856 and was interred in the vaults of the church. He was succeeded by the Rev. Edward (Canon) MacCabe P.P. who, as previously mentioned, finished the exterior of the Church in 1860.* Inside the Church of St. Nicholas of Myra one is immediately struck by the magnificent Pietà and the two angels above and beside the main neoclassical Italian altar, which are the work of the famous Cork sculptor, John Hogan. The altar itself was endowed by Pope Gregory 16th with special privileges and was purchased in Rome. Further statuary is by John Smith. On either side of the centre aisle are stained glass windows sponsored by relatives of loved ones departed; mainly from the studio of Earley & Co. Three windows behind the altar were bricked up to allow the Pietà to be the main focal point.

The works of Nicholas Joseph Crowley (1840) are no longer extant; they were said to adorn the Baptisterium. The present Baptistery is a more recent annex without windows. Presumably, Crowley's stained-glass works were situated in the windows of the north wall and later replaced for some reason. In the Nuptial Chapel, however, many a Dubliner throughout the years has knelt with his bride beneath the work of Harry Clarke's *'Marriage of Our Lady and St. Joseph,'* considered one of the best examples of his work; it was commissioned by Rev. Hayden P.P., in 1828. The doors of the chapel

---

* When Canon MacCabe was transferred to Kingstown. The parish was divided; a line was drawn from Blackpitts through Malpas Street, Lazy lane, Camden Row to Wexford Street. All North of the line remainded in the Francis Street Parish and all South of the line became part of the newly formed Kevin Street parish; the wooden chapel of St.Kevin having being erected on a plot of land secured by the Canon. He became Archbishop of Dublin (1879) and later a Cardinal.

are also the work of Harry Clarke. Looking up one is quite dazzled by the display overhead. The sanctuary ceiling is decorated with a circle of the 12 apostles and in the corners, the four fathers of the Western Church. The ceiling of the nave is decorated with Celtic designs and Christian symbols. Two panels are of particular interest - one showing the Isle of Man coat of arms, and the other commemorating the founding of the Legion of Mary in nearby Myra Hall in 1921. It is the only church in the city to preserve its two sets of communion rails: -
'an interesting relic of 19th century social stratification. The better-off came in the side doors, paid three pence, occupied the front seats and took communion at the altar. The less well-off, came in the back door, paid a penny and took communion half way down the church. Splendid that the ample sanctuary space created for the restored liturgy is so tastefully done in pinks and whites and is located between these two rails.'[xxiv]

Special mention must be made of a loyal servant of the church, Tom Hore, bell-ringer at St. Nicholas of Myra for nearly fifty years. From boyhood, Tom, born in 1851 tolled the bells here and was later sexton:
'He was one who was considered a regular landmark and who figured very largely in the eyes of the parishioners of the old parish, in the heart of the most historic part of Dublin...Ever since childhood, I was one of the favored few acolytes and choristers he would admit to his sanctum, the belfry, where the major part of his time was spent. He revelled in that tower, and I never recall his movements without thinking of Quasimodo and Victor Hugo's description of the turrets of Notre Dame. He was a curious little man who retained a boyish appearance in spite of his years and looked on his duties as being only second in importance to those of an archbishop. He was nothing if not original, I scarcely ever saw him read, and writing he scorned. His favourite relaxation from his duties was to witness a Shakespearian play...When, some years ago, on a Sunday morning we heard with a shock of the sudden death of Canon Daniel (April, 1895), I found him, rope in hand, bowing to the ground, with tears in his eyes,

proclaiming to the parishioners they had lost one of the greatest priests Dublin ever knew...On Christmas Morn, he took particular pride in being the first for many a year to break the stillness of the air with his bell to summon the people for 6 o'clock Mass, by starting three quarters of an hour before the time.'[xxv]

Tom married local girl, Mary Reynolds, the daughter of a nail-maker and the two settled at 67, Francis Street. They had four children. The church-bells tolled for Tom in 1911. Presumably, because he was rarely seen and yet was so often heard, Tom had earned the moniker of "the Phantom."

In recent years Fr. Conleth (Con) Curley P.P.(1993-2005), had a great fondness for the church of St. Nicholas of Myra and undertook the daunting task, in Millennium year, of refurbishing the building. It was badly in need of repair and decoration. The refurbishment was on a large scale consisting of scaffolding up to the ceiling. The plaster walls were flaking and the paintwork discoloured. The church, as it stands today, is very beautiful; largely because of his dedicated efforts. It is a tribute to him. On 26th May 2001, a service was held to celebrate the reopening of the Church . Fr. Curley was a very popular priest who had a way with people, particularly the sick and the youth of the parish. The latter, he encouraged to participate in sporting activities, sport being a subject close to his own heart. He died in August 2005, and was the last person to date to be interred in the vaults, as was his wish..

There is one subject yet to be discussed with relation to the parish of St Nicholas of Myra, and one that raises many an inquiry from those admiring the ceiling panel depicting the coat of arms of the Isle of Man. As old registers here will bear testimony, the Isle of Man was until 1850 included in the diocese of Francis Street. My own research on this has brought me to the Isle of Man and to Francis Coakley, an invaluable source of anything Manx. With her help and further research I have unearthed a forgotten, but most intriguing story.

St. Nicholas of Myra , Francis street, Dublin

Not the airbrushed image, but as it really is- part of a busy urban street.

Panel showing Isle of Man crest

The Church interior.

The Marriage of Our Lady and St. Joseph, by Harry Clarke.

St. Patrick's Cathedral

St. Mary's Castletown, Isle of Man.

St. Nicholas's Parish & Isle of Man

It is said that, since the Reformation, the parishes of the Isle of Man have been linked to Dublin and relied on visiting missionaries for their religious and educational instruction. Successive bishops had used St. Nicholas of Myra as a Pro Cathedral and were in control of these missionaries. Among these priests were, Fr. Molloy O.S.A. an Augustinian and renowned preacher from John's Lane and Fr. Mc Mullen who went there between the years 1798-1805. One of the parish registers of St. Nicholas's lists a baptism on the isle in 1793. But in a more personal way, the connection was with Fr. Matthew Gahan and the Rev. Miles MacPharlan. Here are their stories.

After the tyranny of Henry VIII, and then Oliver Cromwell, few Roman Catholics were left on the Isle of Man. In the early part of the 18th. century only 29 Catholics were listed. Following the 1798 rebellion, many Catholics fled there and the numbers rose to over 200. At this time, as we have already explored, Archbishop Troy had left the St. Nicholas Without site at the former Franciscan chapel in Francis St. and was now in Liffey Street, where he had adopted an old chapel as his new Pro-Cathedral and Mensal Parish. Among his curates was the Rev. Miles MacPharlan. That same year, a certain Major Taubman and the Manx Fencibles were ordered to Dublin to quell the rebellion. Whether spontaneously or by a billeting order, Father MacPharlan surrendered his apartments to the commander and otherwise showed him kindness and hospitality which would one day be rewarded.

In 1803, Father MacPharlan was promoted parish priest of Blanchardstown, or Castleknock, as the parish was then denominated. In order to alleviate unemployment and to promote industrious behaviour he conceived the project of establishing a brick factory and to this enterprise he substantially invested. However, he was soon in debt and to escape imprisonment fled to the Isle of Man, where he resolved to exercise his ministry for the benefit of the Catholic islanders Here he renewed acquaintance with his '98 friend, Major Taubman.

Douglas, Isle of Man, was at that time an obscure fishing village. When mass was celebrated, a parlour of a public house in New Bond Street did duty as a temporary Chapel. If any family of position required the priest's presence on account of sickness, a priest was summoned specially from Dublin. Fr. MacPharlan, with his friend's help, erected the first Catholic chapel, in the year 1813. It was built in a disused quarry on the Castletown road about a mile from Douglas on land granted by Major Taubman, who was proprietor of the neighbouring manor of the Nunnery; formerly the site of St. Brigid's Convent. The chapel was opened in 1814, and a Latin inscription, still preserved on an old stone tablet in St. Mary's, Douglas, records the fact . —

> " To God, Greatest and Best,
> Rev. Miles MacPharlan,
> A Parish Priest near Dublin,
> Restored to its ancient worship
> The Chapel of St. Bridget,
> In the year 1814."

Eventually, his creditors caught up with him and he was obliged to seek refuge in France. The Catholics of the Isle were once more left without a pastor. Once more they had to rely on visiting priests.

Fr. James Francis Kavanagh served in the chapel in Francis Street between 1812-1814 and was on the Isle in 1813. This man, presumably was the same Fr. Kavanagh mentioned in the Dublin registers as having baptized a number of islanders in 1813. The next priest to come here would be the one most readily associated today with the Isle of Man.

Fr Mathew Gahan S.J., was born in Dublin on 7th February, 1782. He entered the Society for the Irish Mission at Hodder House (1805) and, having completed his Noviceship, commenced his Theology at Stonyhurst and finished it at Palermo, where he was ordained Priest, in July, 1810. The Society of Jesus was suppressed by Pope Clement XIV in 1773. Almost forty years later, Fr. Gahan was one of three Jesuits in this new Mission, Fr. Peter Kenny and Fr. William Dinan, being the other two. They took up residence at 3, George's Hill, which had been a Jesuit House before the suppression.

During this time, we have one record of Fr. Gahan's activity which may be of interest. In 1811, he was sent with two nuns from George's Hill Convent to Drogheda, where the townspeople were anxious that a convent should be started "for the better training of the poor girls of the town." Fr. Gahan accompanied Mother Ignatius Doran and Sr. Catherine newly professed, and stayed with them for two weeks.[xxvi]

Fr. Peter Kenny, meanwhile had established Clongowes Wood College on the estate of Castle Browne in County Kildare. In 1814 he was joined by Fr. Gahan, who taught here until 1822 in the capacity of Minister. Then in 1822, he was ordered back to Dublin as Coadjutor to F. Aylmer, at the residence of the Society in Hardwicke Street. At this time he was appointed curate of St. Nicholas Without, where he heard of the plight of the Catholics on the Isle of Man who, without a resident priest, were *"lying like sheep without a Shepherd."*

'Occasionally some two or three Irish priests went across incognito in fishing boats to visit them, and Fr. Gahan took his turn.'[xxvii]

In 1823, accompanied by John Kelly, a schoolteacher, he set sail for the neighboring isle to begin the work for which he is today so fondly remembered. At Castletown, Father Gahan founded a school in 1824, beside the old Chapel of St. Brigid, near Douglas, on the Castletown road. His companion, schoolteacher, John Kelly is said to have presided over "the promiscuous gathering of juvenile islanders." The school comprised both Catholics and Protestants, high and low, rich and poor, all mingled together in the one apartment. Adults, too, were welcomed; the school-fees were bartered for potatoes, apples, cabbages, and useful groceries. The teacher, nicknamed, "Kelly the Roman," was very much the archetypical master who made liberal use of the cane:

'The memories and discipline of the Irish schoolmaster are still graven on the legend-roll of many a Manx homestead. By all accounts,- *A man severe he was, and stern to view.*' [xxviii]

The school was followed, in 1826, by the opening of St Mary's Church in Castletown, which was then the capital. It still stands today, though the roof has been renewed a number of times. He then turned his attention to Douglas and the "miserable" [*] little chapel of Miles MacPharlan in the old quarry a mile outside the town, with leaky roof and where the road was bad; often cited as a cause of preventing many from going to Mass in winter. Clearly, something better was now needed with the increase in the Catholic population.

Fr. Gahan became a resident on the Isle from 1826 to the end of his life. With funds raised from his friends on brief return visits to Dublin, he acquired an old theatre, St. George's Hall, at the corner of Athol Street and Prospect Hill on the island, which was adapted for use as a chapel and school in 1836. This is today the nerve centre of the city of Douglas, but the church, dedicated to St. Francis Xavier no longer exists, having being replaced by the present St. Mary of the Isle Church in 1859, about 100 yards from the original. The Isle of Man parishes, for so long associated with St Nicholas Without, were eventually (1850) included in the diocese of Liverpool. The remainder of Fr. Gahan's life was devoted to the Manx people,

---

* so described, in a letter to Dr. George Oliver, by Father Peter Kenny, S.J., Oct 13th, 1837.

despite many discouragements, all of which he bore with exemplary patience and fortitude. The opening of his church at Douglas, in 1836, was delayed because the Bishop insisted that the sale of MacPharlan's old chapel in the quarry should first be completed; a most unreasonable stance, considering that Fr. Gahan was wholly responsible for the planning, building and fundraising of the new church. By the time the church opened, Fr. Gahan was on his death bed. He had gone out on a visit to the sick and had contracted fever. Fr. Aylmer heard of the bad conditions in which Fr. Gahan was living and went to bring him home to the Jesuit House in Dublin. However, when he arrived, he found the good priest dying. He died on 22nd. February,1837, after five days illness and was buried beside the walls of St. Brendan's Church in the cemetery outside Douglas; a Celtic Irish cross marking the grave. Future generations hailed him as the Irish Apostle of the Isle of Man. His memorial reads:

To the peaceful remembrance of
The Rev. Mathew Joseph Gahan, S.J.
He left his own people in Ireland
to devote himself to the
Salvation of the inhabitants
of the Isle of Man.
He was conspicuous for his piety towards God.
and
Zeal for his neighbour
For kindness towards the poor, for charity
towards all
Amidst the hardships of weak health
He was ever unwearied.
At length after building two
Churches he was struck down by fever
Whilst attending a dying bed
And sweetly expired, February 22,
In the year of Salvation, 1837,
At the age of 56.

Recent Excavations
Behind St. Nicholas of Myra

Described as "a pair of concrete boxes," the most radically unconventional semi detached houses in Dublin were constructed in 2004 at John Dillon street. Architect Tom de Paor had dug into a lot behind the church of St. Nicholas of Myra and in the process made a startling discovery:

"During the excavation we discovered the site had been a burial ground in a 16th-century cholera epidemic," he said. The houses, lighted naturally from above, are essentially buried in a graveyard. These houses " *a mixture of opulence and monasticism"* are ultra modern in design set underground with no windows as such and no doors you can open (sliding door partitions). Included with the house purchase is an archaeological drawing of the Norman layer from which the site was excavated. Steel stairs lead up to the roof terrace, where residents can dine out al fresco with a panoramic view that takes in the parish priest's house, the church's stained glass windows, as well as the apartments on St. Patrick's street. Down below, the buried lower floor is at a depth where human remains (22 bodies) were found and later sent to the National Museum. The property is still classified as church grounds and some of the external planting (silver birch, cherry and mountain ash) is actually on church property.

De Paor's business partner, Jay Bourke, owner of a string of restaurants and bars bought the site eight years ago and put up the money to realise Tom de Paor's quirky vision. An Bord Pleanala turned down the plan twice, forcing it to run four years over deadline, and resulting in the project costing twice its €500,000 budget. As such they were the highest building costs per square foot of any property in Dublin. Most commentators believed that no profit at all was possible and that the only value to the planners would be the media attention generated by de Paor, best known for building a pavilion out of bales of peat briquettes (at the Venice Biennale in

2000). However, in 2006,[*] the first house, whimsically addressed, Zero, John Dillon Street (its twin is addressed Minus One), was sold to Irish rugby international, Shane Horgan for £750,000. Already the buildings are listed, so no alterations can be made.[xxix]

---

[*] De Paor, 38, was named young architect of the year in London in 2003, winning the Corus Building Design competition. The judges describe his work as "playful, funny and profound". Since then he has become one of the most prolific architects in the country, designing residential and commercial scheme in both Ireland and Britain. His most high-profile projects include an angular copper-clad pumphouse in Clontarf, Dublin 3.

Appendix

Isle of Man Baptisms from the Register of St. Nicholas, Francis Street, Dublin

This information is taken from the original parish records (translated from the Latin) and is the total of entries recorded at St. Nicholas.[xxx] Incidentally, the parish records (Dublin) commence in 1742.

1793, December: Patrick Moran of Peter and Maria Dowling. Sponsors, George Dowling and Margaret McEvoy.

1814 July: - Conley of Robert and Anna Hughes, sponsor, James Hughes and Ellen Quin (or Quirke)

James Quin of Henry and Anna Hines. Sponsors, Daniel Rodgers and Ann?

Patrick Breen of Nicholas and Catherine McVay. Sponsors, Pat Cunningham and Ann Quin.

Baptized by J.F. Kavanagh, Vicarius

1813, Insula Mona
Aug. 29th : Margaret Mc Carty of John and Joanne Craig. Sponsors, Daniel Rogan & Maria?

Sept. 4th. George Graham of Edward and Eleanora Farren. Sponsors, Barnabas & Joanna Kelly

Sept. 12th. Elizabeth Mariner of Patrick and Catherine Carron. Sponsors, Tobias & Catherine Francis (Francisco)

Sept 19th. Elizabeth Magreevy of James & Maria Flinn. Sponsors, Barnabas Mc Cullen & Rose Magee.

Sept 26th. Hugo Joseph Carr of Michael & Margaret Doyle. Sponsors, Henry & Maria Rice

Sept. 26th. Daniel Cuffe of Daniel & Margaret Stoale? , Sponsors, James & Ann Duff

Oct. 2nd Alexander Traynor of Denis. Sponsors, Patrick & Ann Traynor.

The Vaults Of St. Nicholas Of Myra Church

Taken from the parish registers some of which are difficult to decipher. I have retained the original spelling. They were recorded at different times according to interment date and according to date order. Additions have been made from the inscriptions on the plaque at the entrance to the vaults.

This church has three vaults each 40 by 20 by 12 feet high

Listed According to Date of Interment:

7th Apr. 1829, Mrs. Hanna O'Connor. She kept the Deal yard in Engine Alley. (Francis McEvoy, Clerk of the Chapel).

2nd Apr. 1829, Miss Mary Purcel, (15 years) Brides Alley.

2nd July 1829, Miss Mary Murray, (18 years) Francis Street.

2nd Sept. 1829, Mr. Mark Ging, (26 years) H. Row, a farmer.

15th Sept. 1829, Mr. Cunningham, (70 years) pipemaker.

10th Nov. 1829 widow Hefferen (80 years).

5th Apr. 1830. Mr. Thomas Ward, (53 years) Kevin Street, near New Street - he kept a Public House.

26th Apr. 1830, Rev. Mr. Richard Kenrick, Parish Priest.

20th Feb. 1830, Mr. Stephen Flanagan, brother Parish Priest.

14th May 1830, Mr. Patrick Byrne, (55 years) Francis Street. Pawn Broker & Cheese Shop.

25th Jun.1830, Mrs. Mary Flanagan, (75 years) laid to rest by her son, Rev. Flanagan, P.P.

8th Sept. 1829, Mr. Cunningham.

1st Jul. 1830, Frederick Kinselo (Kinsella?) 20 years, Pinmaker; his mother keeps a cake shop.

2nd July 1830, Mrs. Bridget Purcel (60 years). Kept a Linen Drapery Shop, No. 33 Francis Street.

13th July1830, Master John George Coleman (15 years) His father kept a Cloth Shop, No.19 Francis Street.

27th Sept 1830, Rev. Mr. Gahan, (57 years) curate in Meath Street Chapel.

5th Oct. 1830 Mrs. Tute, (26 years) James Gate, She kept the Flour Store

6th Dec. 1830, Miss Mary Pennel, (60 years) Marks Alley & Camden Street.

21st Sept. 1830, Patrick Kane, aged three months. His father kept the hair-shop in Francis Street.

7th Jan. I831, Elizabeth Etchingham, aged one year and half. Her father kept a grocer Sloop in Kevin Street opposite Church Lane.

5th Feb. 1831, Rev, Mr. Thomas Joseph Roork, a curate in Francis Street

13th Feb. 1831, Mr. Patrick Doran (70 years). Kept a stall and Shop at No. 2, Francis Street.

23rd May 1831, Patrick Ward, aged 22 years. Son of Mr. Thomas Ward, Blacksmith, 37, Kevin Street.

19th May 1831, John Burke (21) Died 16 May

23rd Feb. 1831, Daniel O' Shoughnessy (34 years). Lived in Kevinsport and kept a public house.

2nd Nov. 1831, Sister Mary Magdalene Donagh (66 years), of the Community of St. Clare, Harold's Cross.

16th Nov.1831, William James Leeson (12 months) Born the 9th Nov. 1830 and died 13 Nov. 1831. Son of John Leeson (Architect).

10th Feb. 1832, Miss Catherine Grovi ? (36 years) -relation Leeson the Architect.

5th March 1832, Mrs. Anne Gilligan,(63 years) servant to Mr. Pimm? the Quayer? (Quaker?) of Ushers Quay. Died 2nd February 1832.

12th Mar. 1832, Mr. Mathew McKeon, (50 years) Linen Draper of Cutpurse Row, near Kevin Street.

24th Mar. 1832, Mrs. Elizabeth Herbert,(80 years) Victualers of Walls Lane. Died 22nd Mar 1832.

27th Mar. 1832, Mr. Thomas Seagrave, (68 years) Chandlery and tobacconist, Upper Kevin Street.

3rd Apr.1832, James Francis Dowling (33 years), Victualler late of Ball Alley, Patrick's Street, Died 31 Mar.

6th May 1832, Robert John Sherlock, (27 years), son of Robert Sherlock of Patrick Street. Died 5 May 1832

10th Jun. 1832, Christopher Joseph Sherlock (30 years), brother of the above R, J. Sherlock. Died 7th June.

13th Jun. 1832, Mrs Mary Moore (51). Died 11th Jun.

23rd Jul. 1832, Mr. Barnaby Kelly (87 years), Tanner formerly of Mill Street removed from the Chapel of Townsend Street. Died 23rd March 1829.

3rd Aug. 1832, Mrs. Annie Butler (31 years), Stephen's Green.

1st Nov. 1832, Master Patrick Kenrick (8 years) son of Mr. Peter Kenrick of Smithfield and nephew of the late Rev. Richard Kenrick of this church, died 31st Oct. 1832.

17th Apr. 1833, Miss Catherine McCormick (95) of Merchants Quay, formerly Marks Alley. Died 14th Apr.

13th Aug. 1834, M. W. Casey, (54 years); this entry from the plaque)

18th Dec. 1834, M. T. Lane (45 years); (this entry from plaque)

18th May 1837, Mrs. Mary Talbot (70 years) of Ardee Street.

26th June 1837, Miss Chari? Healy (28 years) -this entry from the plaque

30th Jun. 1837, Miss E. Harmon (44 years) -this entry from plaque.

18th May 1838, Mrs. Christina Farrell (24 years) of Harold's Cross.

28th Aug. 1833, William Sweeney (57 years) Senior; died at New Bridge.

1st Nov. 1835 Mrs. Roche, (90 years) died Bray, Wicklow.

23rd Jan. 1836, Mrs. Delahide (80 years). Died Rathmines.

1st. April 1836 Mrs. Brownrigg (68 years), Kevin Street.

23rd Jan. 1837, Mrs. Mary Ann Barron (71 years) Harcourt Street.

24th Jan. 1837, Miss Margaret Byrne (16 years), Kimmage.

1st Dec. 1836, Mrs. Cath Murphy (17 years), Francis Street.

26th Jan. 1837, Mr. James Lawler (57 years), Spittalsfield.

18th Mar. 1837, Edward Leeson (7mts.), Clare Street.

28th Apr. 1837, Mary O'Callaghan (42 years), 125, Francis Street.

6th Jan. 1831, Thomas Redmond. Aged 77 years.

12th Mar. 1831, Teresa Mary C. Moore (14 years)

6th Feb. 1834, Michael Dowdal (34 years).

28th. Feb. 1834, Anne Larkin (28 years).
3rd Jul. 1837, Rev. Mr. Paul Long (82 years).

9th. Aug. 1837, Mrs. Ellen Lynch (30 years).

9th Aug. 1834, Rev. Jos. Curran (38 years).

28th Sept. 1837, Mrs. Annie Dune (36 years).

28th Feb. 1837, Thomas. Woodcock (31 years)

8th Sept. 1829, Mr. Cunningham.

19th. Feb. 1837, Mr. Peter Ffrench

13th Feb. 1834, Mrs. Elen Grove.

7th Feb. Mrs. Margaret Dowdal (66 years), Harold's Cross.

27th Feb. 1834. -? Gabe, child of Mr.- ? Gabe (McCabe?) Ushers Island.

14th Apr. 1834, Mrs. McDaniel. Age?

28th. Jun. 1834, Mr. William Woodcock (63 years).

7th Aug. 1834, John Doyle age. ?

26th. Sept. 1834, James Boylan.

2nd Jan. 1835, Catherine Casey (33 years).

13th Jan. 1835, Mrs. Margaret Dodd (50 years).

18th Nov. 1837, Rev. Richard Murray. Died 3 o'clock, 17th Nov. aged 38

7th. Jan. 1838, Mrs. Ellen McLoughlin.

10th Mar.1838, Rev. Patrick Doyle(34 years), Rathmines Parish.

16th Mar.1838, Owen Ryan (44 years)
6th Apr. 1838, Catherine Coppinger (33 years).

11th Jun. 1838, Jn ? Reddy. Kevins ?, (60 years).

31st. Jul.1838, Peter Dowdal, Harold's Cross (77 years).

19th. Aug. 1838, Miss Margaret Birmingham (14 years) Francis Street.

9th Apr. 1839, Mrs. Margaret O'Brien (64 years), 30 Leeson Street.

23rd Dec. 1839, Mrs. Margaret Legrane (70 years). 1, Upper Kevin Street.

17th Feb. 1840, Robert Sherlock (72 years). 5, Patrick Street.

4th Mar. 1840, Walter Byrne(64 years); 12 Skinners Alley.

21st Apr. 1840, Mrs. Alicia Ward (52 years). 35, Upper Kevin Street.

11th Sept. 1840, Rev. Robert Malone (78 years). Died 9th Sept. New Row.

17th Sept. 1840, William Dowling, Francis Street (52 years)

19th Oct. 1840, Mrs. Sarah Frances Burke (29 years) Camden Street.

15th. Nov. 1840, Mrs. Mary Anne Cullen (22 years), daughter of - ?Carroll, New Ross.

4th Dec.1840, Miss Ellen Leeson. Aged 5 years.

16th Feb. 1841, Mrs. Ann Ryan (43 years), Rathmines.

4th Oct. 1841, Walter Burke (79 years), Ardee Street.

31st Dec. 1841, Mrs. Mary Dowling (24 years) Francis Street.

27th Feb. 1842, Mrs. Margaret Dowling (22 years), Francis Street.

5th Apr. 1842, Mrs. Margaret Greene (24 years) -Woodcock's family vault.

Listed According to Date of Death

1828, Mrs. Wordont ?Brought from the Paupers Register.

2nd Aug. 1842, Mr. Timothy Burke (31 years), Camden Street.

2nd Sept. 1842, Laurence Neary, (45 years) Little Ship Street.

12th Dec. 1842, John Caffrey, Summer Street (72 years).

18th Mar. 1843, John Henry Caffrey (43 years), Summer Street.

20th Sept. 1843, Annie Orr (55 years), New Street.

? Jun. 1 844, -? O'Bricn, 92 St. Stephens Green.

8th Mar. 1844, Michael Francis Coppinger (43 years), Drumcondra.

26th Mar. 1844, Miss Mary Anne Melody (65 years), Rathmines.

19th Jun. 1844, Mrs. Mary Teresa Caffrey, Summer Street.

7th Aug. 1844, Peter Kendrick (68 years), Smithfield.

8th Sept 1844, John Delaney (68 years), Rathfarnham,

3rd Oct. 1844, Miss Sarah Caffrey (18 years), Summer Street.

6th Nov. 1844, Miss Annie Malloy (67 years), New Row.

19th Dec.1844, Michael James Lalor (16 years). Adelaide Road.

31st Dec. 1844, Miss Ellen Groves (26 years), Clare Street.

2nd Feb. 1845, Mary Doyle (18 years), Francis Street,

29th Jan. 1846, Bartholomew Bourke Mahon (40/5 years) of the Liberty.

6th Feb. 1846, Mrs. Teresa Leeson (49 years), Clare Street.

15th Feb. 1846 Patrick Mc Loughlin (27 years), Francis Street.

27th Jul. 1846, Master John Walsh, Dean Street, aged a few days.

19th Sept. 1846, Patrick Larkin (60 years)

11th Oct. 1846, Thomas Legrane (30 years), Harcourt ?

16th Mar. 1847, Joseph Henry Corr (2 years). Blacklen ? Street.

16th Apr. 1847, Mrs. Mary Anne Kelly (66 years). Harold's Cross.

14th May 1847, Mrs. Margaret Sweeny (62 years), 58 Camden Street.

31st Aug. 1847, Master John Currishly (8 mths), infant relative of Mr. Reily.

5th Oct. 1847, Miss Mary Ryan (18 years), Kilmacud.

14th Feb. 1848, Laurence Mooney (55 years), Pill Lane.

14th Apr. 1848, Joshua Egghead (40), Coombe.

14th Mar. 1851, Mrs. John Caffrey (73 years), Summer Street.

19th Aug. 1851, John Horan (38 years), attorney, Aungier Street.

12th Sept. 1851, Mrs. Ann Cook (52 years). Harcourt Street.

25th. Mar. 1852, Miss Mary Dowling (70 years). Francis Street.

10th Mar. 1853, Mrs. Mary Murphy (47 years): Francis Street; Grocer,

Listed According to Date of Interment:

8th. Jun. 1853, Mrs. Agnes Byrne (70 years). Westly Terrace.

22nd Oct. 1853, Mrs. Judith Nowlan Kinsella, (76 years) Mountain View Avenue, Harold's Cross.

13th. Jan. 1854, John Carberry Leeson (55 years). 25, Clare Street.

6th Sept. 1854, Miss Eliza Walsh (10 years). Dean Street.

16th Oct. 1854, Patrick Grace? (86 years) the Coombe.

19th Oct. 1854, Elizabeth Lalor (61 years). Spittalfields.

9th Feb. 1855 John O'Brien (60 years), esq. Brother to Serj. O'Brien of 92, St. Stephen's Green. Died 6th.Feb.

19th Apr. 1855, Miss Teresa Lalor (28 years). Spittalfields.

29th Apr. 1856, Rev. Dr. Flanagan, P.P. (73 years)
Died at Hormonley, Rathgar. Died 26 April.

2nd May 1856, Miss Catherine Doyle (23 years). Clanbrasil Street.

15th. Feb. 1868, Mrs. Anne Seagrave (87 years), 92 Stephen's Green. Mother-in-law to Judge O'Brien.

3rd Dec. 1857, Mr. William Dean Butler (63 years), of Stephens Green. Died 28th Nov.

17th Jan. 1860, Mrs. Elizabeth Frances Lalor (33 years) of Spitalfields and Kingstown. Died 15th. Jan.

21st Dec. 1860, Mrs. Ellen O'Brien , Pembroke Place. Died 19th. December,

.3rd June 1868, Mr. John Murphy (73 years). Francis Street. Died 3 May.

8th Sept. 1868, Miss Ellen Kinchella (39 years), sister-in-law to Mr. John Murphy of Francis Street.

4th. Nov. 1869, Revd. James Hichey (57 years), C. C., Church of St. Nicholas, Francis Street. Died 1st Nov.1869.

11th Apr. 1870, Rev. Martin Barlow (47 years), P.P. of St. Kevins. Died 8th April 1870,

20th. Jan. 1871, Mr. John Murphy, Junior, son of above John Murphy.

5th Apr. 1871, Edward Frederic Murphy (36 years), son of Mr. John Murphy, Francis Street.

9th Jan. 1872, William Augustin Murphy (34 years), son of same John Murphy.

16th Sept. 1873, Mrs. Catherine Delany (77 years), Air Park, Rathfarnham.

7th Apr. 1877, Miss Eliza Mallay (73 years). Died, 4 Apr. 1877.

14th Jul. 1880, Mrs. Hanna Mary Horan (73 years), Rathfelh ?

22nd Nov. 1880, Joanna Murphy (41 years), Roebuck.

2nd Jan. 1882, Right Honorable James O'Brien (50 years), second justice of the Court of Queens County, 92, Stephens Green. Born, 27th Feb.1831. Died 29th Dec. 1881.

7th Apr. 1895, Very Rev. Canon Daniel, PP. (this entry from plaque)

22nd May 1905, James O'Brien (50 years), son of O'Brien above; 94, Lr. Baggott Street. Died 22nd. May.

30th Jul. 1993, Very Rev. Desmond O'Brien, PP. (this entry from plaque)

26th July 2000, Christina DeVesey. (this entry from plaque).

9th Aug. 2005, **Very Rev. Conleth Curley, P.P.**

65

Sources & Notes

MSS. Dublin Chapels, Vol. II, p53: The British Museum

A History of the City of Dublin: John Thomas Gilbert, 1854

An Historical Guide to the City of Dublin, George Newenham Wright, 1821

Dublin Churches, Peter Costello

Dublin, The City Within the Grand and Royal Canals and The Circular Road with the Phoenix Park, Christine Casey

St Patrick's and Nicholas Without, Saturday Magazine, 1833

New York Times,- Dublin Design- Virginia Gardiner, Jan. 5th 2006

St. Nicholas of Myra Church, Paddy Duffy, Village Magazine

St. Nicholas of Myra and Its Two Architects, An Historical and Architectural Survey, by Millie Lawler

Collections Towards Illustrating the Biography of the Scotch, English, and Irish Members of the Society of Jesus: 'Fr Mathew Gahan,' Rev. Dr. George Oliver. London, 1838

Ireland and the Isle of Man, by Rev. Dean Walsh, Rector St. Mary's Douglas. Revised and enlarged by Rev. N. Donnelly, The Catholic Truth Society of Ireland, Dublin,1903

The Catholic Church and The Isle of Man, W .S. Dempsey

Fr. Mathew Gahan SJ, 1782-1837, Dominic Dowling
Catholic Life pp18/9 Sept 2007

A Valiant Dublin Woman,-The Story of Georges Hill   Convent, Roland Burke Savage, S.J.

The Dublin City Churches of Church of Ireland, H.A Wheeler & M.J. Craig

Around the Churches, the Stories of the Churches in St. Patrick's Cathedral Group of Parishes, by John Crawford, Vicar of St. Patrick's Cathedral

Dr. John Carpenter, by Dr. Brian Mac Giolla Phadraig
Dublin Historical Record, Vol. XXX, No 1. Pp 10-11.

Records & History of the Church of St. Nicholas of Myra, Francis Street: article by G.H. O'Reilly, MA FRSAI, the Genealogical Record, Dun Laoghaire, 2003

The Second City, A Portrait of Dublin 1700-1760, Patrick Fagan, Branar, Dublin 1986

Dublin Penny Journal, 1832 and *The Freeman's Journal* 1840

Dublin 1660-1860, Maurice Craig; Allen Figgis, Dublin, 1969

A Short History of Some Dublin parishes: Part VI. Rev. N. Donnelly

The History of Ireland, Commencing With Its Earliest Period, To The Great Expedition Against Scotland: Thomas Moore Philadelphia, Lea & Blanchard, 1843

The Making of Ireland, From Ancient Times to the Present: James Lydon, 1998, Routledge

Dublin City Walls and Defenses, Dublin City Council 2006

St. Patrick's Cathedral Dublin, guide book: Published by Scala Ltd

St. Luke's Conservation Plan: Dublin City Council, 2005

A New Picture of Dublin: Comprehending a History of the City: John James McGregor - 1821

The Catholic Bulletin, 1912

Excursions Through Ireland; Thomas Cromwell, 1820

Ireland and Her Churches, James Godkin, 1860

History of the Archbishops of Dublin,: E.A. D' Alton, Dublin, 1838

Travels in Holland,: The United Provinces, England, Scotland, and Ireland, William Brereton 1844

One way Street And other Writings, Walter Benjamin 1979

Oxford Dictionary of National Biography: H.C.G. Matthew, Brian Howard Harrison, 2004

The Irish Times, April 28th. 2005

The Sunday Times, July 9th. 2006

Illustrations Used

Colour Inserts:
St. Nicholas ,by Earley & Co: courtesy of   St. Nicholas's Parish Church
St Nicholas Within, Photo by Liam O' Meara
The Marriage Our Lady and St. Joseph: St Nicholas's Parish Church
St. Nicholas of Myra 2008, John Brogan , Liberties Living Heritage
Ceiling Panel, St Nicholas of Myra: John Brogan, ibid
St. Mary's Castletown: Francis Coakley/Dominic Dowling
Church interior: St. Nicholas's Parish Church
St. Patrick's Cathedral: Liberties Living Heritage

Black & White:
St Nicholas Within: *The Gentleman's Magazine,* 1786
Archbishop Richard Whately: from a 19th. century book: author and artist
unknown; copyright expired; taken from Wikipedia
Dublin 1610, from map by John Speed
St Nicholas Without: *The Penny Journal,* Vol. 1, Dec.29, 1832 (pp213)
The Cabbage Garden, (1) & (2) : The Liberties Living Heritage
The Lady Chapel: from *St. Patrick's Cathedral Dublin,* Guide Book
St Luke's: (1)The Representative Church Body
St Luke's; (2) The Liberties Living Heritage
Silken Thomas's siege of the city: *Histoire of Irelande,* Raphael Holinshed,
1577; *Dublin City Walls and Defenses,* Dublin City Council 2006
Silken Thomas renouncing allegiance to VIII: By H Warren.

Stained Glass Windows Of Present Church

Left of Centre Aisle:
St. Patrick- in memory of Robert Staples, Curate of the Church
St. Joseph- in memory of Thomas Rafter, 106, the Coombe.
St. Nicholas, to whom the church is dedicated
All of the above by Early & Co., 1902.

Right of Centre Aisle
St. Francis- in memory of Sarah Gibney
St. Theresa- in memory of Theresa Byrne, died 1901
St. Michael- in memory of Rev. Canon Daniel, pastor of Church
1, above by Kevin Kelly, Abbey Stained Glass, 1991
2 & 3, Earley & Co.

North Transept
The Ascension - in Memory of Ann Seagrave, 1869
The Holy Family- in memory of Terence O' Reilly, 1883

South Transept
Thomas a Becket - in memory of Thomas Greally
The Resurrection - in memory of Mary Sweetman, 1862
The Immaculate Conception- in memory of Wm. Kelly

Nuptial Chapel
The Marriage of Our Lady & St. Joseph- sponsor Mary Byrne
By Harry Clarke, 1928

Altar Left
Agony in the Garden, 1850

Altar Right
The Crucifixion- in memory of Mary Murphy. 1850.